Strange Stories

I Talk You Talk Press

CONTENTS

STORY 1: SEE YOU SOON

Janet is the owner of a small company. The office is in the centre of a city. At night, when Janet works late, she always locks the front office door.

It is 9:00pm and she is still working. The other three workers, Kevin, Dave and Anna, have gone home. Now, she is sitting in her room at the back of the office. She is writing a report on her computer.

She hears a noise. It sounds like someone is walking in the office.

What's that? There is no one here. I am alone. The door is locked. Maybe a window is open. Maybe it is the wind, she thinks.

She stands up and walks out of her room. She looks around the main office. No one is there. She goes to the windows. The windows are closed. It is October, and it is cold at night.

She goes back into her room and sits down.

Maybe the sound was from outside, she thinks. *Or maybe I am tired. I worked hard today. I should go home soon.*

Then, her computer makes a noise. It is an email. She looks at the name.

---Henry---

Henry? Who is Henry? she thinks.

Then she looks at the subject.

---To Janet from Henry---

Henry? I don't know anyone called Henry.

She clicks on the email and reads the message.

---You didn't check the kitchen.---

1

Suddenly, Janet feels very cold. She runs to the window and looks outside. The city is dark, but there are lights from other buildings.

Is someone watching me? Someone in another building? Is someone watching me and sending me emails?

She closes the blinds so no one can see into her office. She sits down and looks at the mail again.

The mail was sent to my personal email. Not the company email. My personal email is private. Only my friends know my personal email address. Who is it? Is this a joke?

Then, she hears a noise. It is the kitchen door closing.

She feels very frightened.

Someone is in the kitchen! What should I do? Should I check the kitchen? No, there might be a dangerous person there. I have to call the police.

Janet picks up the phone and calls the police.

"Hello? I need help. Someone is in my office kitchen. Someone is watching me! Please come quickly!"

About fifteen minutes later, two policemen come to her office. She runs out of her room and to the front door of the office. She unlocks it.

She tells the policemen about the strange noise and the email. The policemen open the kitchen door. It is dark. One of the policemen switches on the light.

They look in the kitchen. There is no one there.

"There is no one here," says the policeman.

"But, I heard a noise…and the email…" says Janet.

The policemen walk into Janet's room and look at the email on her computer.

"It is strange," says one of the policemen. "But the door is locked, and the windows are closed. No one is here. Maybe someone is watching you in another building. Close the blinds at night, so no one can see you."

"I don't want to stay here tonight. I will go home now," says Janet.

She switches off her computer and puts her coat on. The policemen wait for her. She picks up her bag, and switches off the lights. They leave the office and Janet locks the door.

"Take care," says one of the policemen. "And call us again if you need us."

"Thank you," says Janet. She walks to the car park, gets in her car, and drives home.

The next morning, Janet goes to the office.

Should I tell the other staff about last night? No, they will think I am crazy, she thinks. *And I don't want them to worry.*

She switches on her computer and opens her email inbox. There are no more emails from Henry.

Janet has a busy day. She has many meetings with customers, and is out of the office most of the day. When she gets back to the office, she has a lot of work to do.

I don't want to stay in the office late tonight, she thinks. *But I have to finish my work.* At around 6:00pm, the other workers go home. Janet closes the blinds on all the windows and locks the front door. She checks the kitchen and the bathroom.

No one is here, and no one can get into the office, she thinks. *It is safe.*

She goes into her room and starts working. At about 8:00pm, she stops and thinks,

I would love a cup of coffee.

Then, she looks up.

I can smell coffee, she thinks. *That is strange. Why can I smell coffee?*

There is a strong smell of coffee. She opens the door. The smell of coffee is coming from the kitchen.

This is crazy, she thinks.

Then, her computer makes a noise.

An email has come, she thinks.

She walks to her desk and looks at her computer.

Henry! It is an email from Henry! she thinks.

She clicks on it and reads it.

---Would you like a cup of coffee?---

Janet looks at the words for a long time. She feels very frightened. She cannot move.

What is this? she thinks. *I have to go into the kitchen. I have to find this person. But maybe the person is dangerous. Should I call the police again?*

She sits down at her desk.

If I call the police, what can I say? I can smell coffee in my office? Please come quickly! The police will think I am crazy! I will look in the kitchen. I have to look.

Very slowly and quietly, she walks to the kitchen. The smell of coffee is very strong. She opens the door. It is dark in the kitchen. She switches the light on. There is no one there, but the coffee maker is on, and there is a fresh cup of coffee next to the coffee maker.

She looks around. *Who made the cup of coffee?*

"Who are you? Where are you?" she asks.

There is no answer. She walks to the cup and looks at it.

Fresh coffee. It looks good, she thinks. She picks it up and smells it. *It smells good too. But, who made it?*

She drinks a little of the coffee. It tastes good. She drinks some more.

This coffee is delicious! she thinks. *This is very strange, but I will drink the coffee.*

She takes the coffee back to her room and looks at the email from Henry. She clicks "Reply" and types:

---*Thank you, Henry. The coffee is very nice.*---

A few seconds later, she gets another email.

---*You are welcome!*---

---*Who are you?*--- she types.

She waits, but there is no answer.

Every night after that, she hears the coffee machine. Then, she gets an email.

---*Your coffee is ready!*---

Every night she goes into the kitchen and takes her coffee. Then, she sends an email.

---*Thank you for the coffee Henry!*---

Then she gets a reply:

---*You're welcome!*---

Then, one night, she gets this message:

---*There is a surprise with your coffee.*---

She goes into the kitchen, and there is a chocolate cake next to the cup of fresh coffee.

She goes back into her office and sends an email.

---*Thank you for the cake. I am very hungry. I need something to eat!*---

A few seconds later, she gets a reply.

---*I'm glad you like it!*---

After that, there is a cake with the coffee every night.

Then, one night she gets this message:

---*There is a big surprise with your coffee and cake!*---

What is it? she thinks.

She goes into the kitchen. Next to the coffee and cake are twelve red roses.

She looks at them for a long time. Then she says, "Who are you Henry? Who are you? Where are you?"

There is no answer.

She writes an email.

---*Please tell me. Who are you? Where are you?*---

A few seconds later, she gets a reply.

---*You will see me soon! I love you!*---

She laughs and types:

---*I love you too!*---

She puts the flowers in a vase in her office.

The next morning, Kevin comes into the office. He sees the roses.

"Red roses! Who are they from?" he asks.

"They are from my friend, Henry," says Janet.

"That's romantic. I think he likes you!" says Kevin. "When did he bring them?"

"Er…last night," says Janet.

I can't tell Kevin about the cake and coffee. He will think I am crazy. Maybe I am crazy, she thinks.

The next night, Janet does not get an email. She waits. She cannot smell coffee.

Where is my coffee? she thinks.

She sends an email to Henry.

---*No coffee and cake today?*---

A few minutes later, she gets a reply.

---*No, because today, I'd like to meet you.*---

Janet types:

---*Meet me? Are you coming here?*---

Henry replies:

---*No, you are coming to see me.*---

Janet types:

---*Where?*---

Henry replies:

---*There is a coffee shop across the road. Go there now.*---

Janet stands up and goes to the window. She looks out of the window at the coffee shop.

Is Henry in the coffee shop? she thinks.

She sends another message.

---*Are you in the coffee shop?*---

5

A reply comes.

---*Come now!*---

Janet puts her coat on. She types:

---*OK, see you soon.*---

Henry replies:

---*Yes, see you very soon!*---

Janet walks out of the office. She is excited and nervous.

This is crazy, she thinks.

She is not looking at the road. She is looking at the coffee shop across the road. There are many people in the coffee shop.

Who is Henry? she thinks. *Is he the man sitting next to the window? Or the man sitting at the counter?*

Janet doesn't see the bus coming down the road. She walks across the road. People are shouting at her.

"Stop!"

"Don't walk!"

"There is a bus!"

But it is too late. The bus hits Janet.

At the same time, an email arrives in Janet's inbox.

---*Welcome to my world.*---

STORY 2: THE BOAT

Rodrigo is on vacation with his mother and father. They are staying in a house next to the beach. They arrived at the house this morning. Rodrigo wants to play on the beach, but he cannot. It is raining heavily.

His father puts the TV on and they watch the weather report.

"There is a storm coming," says his father. "The weather will be very bad tonight, but from tomorrow, it will be nice."

"Let's drive into the village and get some food for dinner," says his mother.

They get into the car and drive along the sea road. Ten minutes later, they arrive in the village. Next to the harbour, there are many fishing boats.

"Fishing boats!" says Rodrigo. "I want to see the fishing boats in the sea!"

"The weather is too bad for the fishermen to go fishing today. Maybe you can see them tomorrow," says his mother.

They go into the small supermarket.

"What do you want to eat tonight?" asks Rodrigo's mother.

"I want to eat beans and rice!" says Rodrigo.

They buy food for dinner and some bread and yoghurt for breakfast the next morning.

The cashier asks, "Are you staying in the house next to the beach?"

"Yes, we are," says Rodrigo's mother.

"There is a storm coming. It will be very noisy tonight. The wind will be very strong," says the cashier. She smiles at Rodrigo. "But after tonight, it will be sunny every day. So you can enjoy your holiday."

Rodrigo smiles. "I want to swim in the sea," he says.

They go back to the house. It is very windy, and the sea is very noisy.

"Look at the sea!" shouts Rodrigo. "The waves are very high!"

"And this rain is very heavy! Come on! Hurry!" says his father.

They take the shopping bags out of the car and run into the house.

While he is waiting for his dinner, Rodrigo sits next to the window and listens to the sea. It is dark, so he cannot see anything. He thinks about tomorrow.

I'll go swimming, I'll play on the beach, I'll have an ice cream, I'll...

"Dinner is ready!" shouts his mother.

They eat dinner and watch TV.

"The wind is so noisy! I cannot hear the TV very well!" says Rodrigo.

His father looks at the clock.

"It's time for you to go to bed. It's noisy, but we had a long drive today, so you are tired. You will sleep well."

Rodrigo says good night to his mother and father and goes to his room.

He reads a little, and then he switches the light off. He falls asleep very quickly.

Rodrigo feels very wet and cold. He is in the water. He is trying to swim, but he cannot. The sea is very rough.

"Help! Help!"

He can hear men shouting.

"Help! Help!"

It is very dark.

"I can't see you!" he shouts.

"Rodrigo! Rodrigo!" Someone is shouting to him.

"I'm here! Can you see me? Help!" he shouts.

He opens his eyes. Someone is shaking him. He is in bed, and his mother and father are looking at him. They look very worried.

"Rodrigo! Rodrigo! Are you OK?" says his mother. "Why are you so wet? Have you been outside? And what is this?"

His mother is holding an old piece of wood. There are two words on the piece of wood. Rodrigo reads them. *High Wind.*

"It's from the boat!" says Rodrigo. "I was on the boat! The boat's name is *High Wind!* Quick! We have to help the men! They are in the water! They will die!"

"But Rodrigo, there is no boat outside!" says his mother. "You are dreaming!"

"He was sleepwalking!" says his father. "Rodrigo, while you were sleeping, you walked outside and went into the water. You picked up this piece of wood from the beach."

"But I was on the boat! And I heard the men! They were shouting for help! Then suddenly, I was in the water too!" says Rodrigo. "Look! My clothes are wet!"

"You were sleepwalking. It was a dream," says his father. "There is no boat. And the sea is very loud. It is too noisy to hear voices!"

"But I heard them! I did!" shouts Rodrigo. "Please go and look! Please look for the men!"

Rodrigo's mother and father look at each other.

"OK, I'll go and look," says his father.

His father gets dressed, and takes a torch outside. A few minutes later, he comes back.

"There is nothing there. You were dreaming," he says.

"But I was on the boat!"

"There are no fishing boats out at sea. All the fishing boats are in the harbour. We saw them when we went to the supermarket. No boats will go out in this storm! You were dreaming! Go back to sleep!" says his mother.

His father checks the front door of the house. It is locked. He takes the key into the bedroom and puts it under his pillow.

Rodrigo cannot get out of the house now, he thinks.

Rodrigo's mother changes his bed sheets, and Rodrigo puts on a clean t-shirt and shorts. He gets into bed.

I wasn't dreaming, he thinks. *I was on the boat. And I heard the men. Why don't they believe me?*

The next morning, Rodrigo wakes up at 7:30am. It is very quiet. He gets up and opens the curtains. It is very sunny. The sea is very calm.

The storm has gone, he thinks. *I can play on the beach today.*

Then, he remembers the boat. He looks at the piece of wood next to his bed.

It was not a dream, he thinks. *I have the name of the boat here.*

He has breakfast with his mother and father.

"Did you sleep OK after your dream?" asks his mother.

"It was not a dream. I was on the boat and I heard the men," he says. "And I have the piece of wood with the boat name on it."

"Let's finish breakfast and go into the village," says his mother. "We can ask someone about the boat called *High Wind*."

They get into the car and drive to the village. At the harbour, they see some fishermen cleaning their boats. They get out of the car and take the piece of wood to the fishermen.

"Excuse me," says Rodrigo's father. "We are staying in the house next to the beach. We found this piece of wood in the sea. Is it from a fishing boat?"

The fishermen look at it.

"*High Wind*! I don't believe it!" says one of the fishermen. "This boat sank in a storm about a hundred years ago. My grandfather told me about it. He was a young boy at the time. He heard the men shouting 'Help! Help!' But no one could help the men. The storm was too bad. All the men died. Where did you find it?"

Rodrigo's mother and father look at Rodrigo.

"I was on the boat," says Rodrigo.

"He was sleepwalking and dreaming last night," says his father.

The fisherman looks at Rodrigo.

"What is your name?" he asks.

"Rodrigo Herrera," says Rodrigo.

The fisherman doesn't say anything. He looks at Rodrigo for a long time.

"What is it?" says Rodrigo's father.

"A young boy was on the *High Wind*. He was only eleven years old. He died in the water. It was very sad."

"I'm eleven," says Rodrigo.

The fisherman looks at him. "And the boy's name was Rodrigo Herrera..."

STORY 3: THE TAXI DRIVER

It is Halloween night. Suzie and Chantelle are university students. They have been to a Halloween party. They had a very good time. Suzie is wearing a ghost costume. Chantelle is wearing a witch costume. It is 11:30pm. The party has finished. Suzie and Chantelle are waiting for a taxi in the centre of the city. There are many other people waiting for taxis. Suzie and Chantelle have been waiting for thirty minutes.

"I'm so cold!" says Chantelle. "This witch costume is very thin."

"I'm cold too. There are many parties tonight," says Suzie. "It will be difficult to get a taxi. All the taxis are busy. What should we do? Shall we start walking home?"

"I'm wearing high heels. It is difficult to walk far," says Chantelle.

Suzie looks at Chantelle's high heels. "You're right. But maybe if we start walking, we can find a taxi on the street."

"Yes, maybe. And it's too cold to wait here. Let's go."

Suzie and Chantelle start to walk home. It starts to rain.

"I want to walk faster, but I can't!" says Chantelle. "I hope we see a taxi!"

The young women live about a forty-minute walk from the city centre. Some cars pass, but they are not taxis.

"Come on taxi! Please! Come down this street! Take us home!" says Suzie.

Just then, they see a car with a light on top. The car is coming down the street.

"Look!" says Chantelle. "I think that is a taxi!"

"I can't believe it!" says Suzie. "The taxi heard me!"

The young women laugh.

Suzie puts her hand up and walks to the side of the road.

"Stop! Stop!" she says.

The taxi stops next to them.

They look through the window at the driver.

"Wow!" says Suzie. "Look at the driver! He is wearing a Halloween costume! He is wearing a skeleton costume!"

"Cool costume!" says Chantelle.

"Can you take us to Coral Street, please?" asks Suzie.

The driver nods his head, but he doesn't say anything.

"Thank you so much. We are so glad to see you!" says Chantelle.

They get in the back of the taxi and the taxi starts to move.

"Were you busy tonight?" asks Suzie.

The driver doesn't answer.

"I like your costume," says Chantelle.

Again, the driver doesn't say anything.

Suzie starts to laugh.

She says to Chantelle quietly, "It is Halloween, so he wants to be scary. He wants us to be scared. So he is wearing a costume and he doesn't say anything."

Chantelle laughs. "Yeah, I think you are right."

Then, the driver starts to drive faster. The girls look at each other.

"Excuse me," says Chantelle. "Can you slow down, please?"

The driver doesn't say anything.

"Chantelle," says Suzie. "Look out of the window. Coral Street is in the south of the city. We are going north. The sea is on our left side. It should be on our right side."

Chantelle looks out of the window.

"You're right!" she says.

She shouts to the driver, "Where are you going? Stop! Stop now!"

But the driver doesn't stop. He drives faster and faster.

The girls scream, "Stop! Stop! You are going to kill us!"

The driver turns right, and the taxi goes down a dark and quiet road. The road is very narrow, and there are trees on both sides of the road. The taxi is going very fast.

"Let's call the police," says Suzie quietly.

"We have no time. If we don't stop the driver now, he will crash. I have a plan," says Chantelle very quietly. "I am sitting behind him so

I can't get to the steering wheel. Can you climb into the front passenger seat?"

"I think so," says Suzie.

"OK. Please try, Suzie. When you are in the front, I will put my belt around his neck. I will pull very hard. Take the steering wheel and try to keep us on the road.

"But I can't drive," says Suzie.

"But we have to do something. We must try. Take the steering wheel and pull the handbrake on. The car will slow down. Then maybe we can open the doors and jump out."

"OK," says Suzie. "Let's try."

Suzie climbs into the front of the taxi. It is very strange. The driver does not look at her. The driver doesn't say anything.

"After three," says Chantelle. "Three, two, one, go!"

Chantelle throws her belt over the driver's head. She pulls hard. Suzie puts her hand out to hold the steering wheel.

But Chantelle screams, "His head! His head! It's…!"

The man's head falls from his neck, and onto the floor.

Suzie stops holding the steering wheel.

"Suzie! The tree!"

The car hits the tree very hard, and everything becomes quiet.

The next day, a TV news reporter and a camera man are standing next to the tree on the road. The tree is damaged. The reporter looks into the camera and starts to speak:

"Last night, at around midnight, a taxi crashed into this tree. There were two young women in the taxi. They were both university students. One woman was wearing a ghost costume, and the other was wearing a witch costume. Police also found a plastic skeleton in the car. Police think the young women bought the skeleton in a costume shop and took it to a Halloween party.

"A friend of the young women was at the party last night. She told police the two young women planned to take a taxi home.

"The owner of the taxi was Max Bearcroft. A woman found Mr Bearcroft lying on the road at about eleven thirty last night. The woman called an ambulance. Mr Bearcroft died in the ambulance on the way to the hospital. Doctors think he had a heart attack. Mr Bearcroft was a driver for Premium One Taxis. Premium One Taxis sent another driver to get Mr Bearcroft's taxi, but it was not there.

"The police think the young women took Mr Bearcroft's taxi. But they have many questions. The young women lived in Coral Street in the south of the city, so why did they drive north?

"How did the women drive the car? The women's friends told police they could not drive, and there were no driver's licenses in their wallets. And another question is this: Why was the plastic skeleton in the driver's seat when the car crashed? The police may never find the answers to the questions. When they came to the place of the accident, the young women were already dead."

STORY 4: APARTMENT 409

After he finishes university, Ken Fujimoto gets a job with a car company. It is in a city far from his hometown, so his new boss says he will help Ken find an apartment. Before he starts his new job, Ken's boss sends him an email

---I found an apartment for you. It is in an old apartment building. The apartment is small, but it is close to our office, and it is cheap.---

The first night in his new city, Ken stays in a hotel near the railway station. The next day his new boss, Mr Matsui, takes him to see the apartment. Ken likes it very much. It is on the fourth floor of an old apartment building. There is one large room with a kitchen, and a bathroom. Outside is a balcony.

I can dry my clothes and put my garbage on the balcony, thinks Ken.

"It is good for one person," says Ken to Mr Matsui. "It is very convenient. Thank you for finding it for me."

"You are welcome," answers Mr Matsui. "It is difficult to find cheap apartments in this city. I think I was lucky to find this one."

Ken moves into apartment 409 on a Friday, at the beginning of April. He is pleased.

I have the weekend free to buy the things I need, and to arrange my apartment.

A small truck comes on Saturday morning with a desk, a chair, a bookcase, and other things for the apartment. Ken's mother sent them from Ken's hometown. Ken goes out to buy a rice cooker and curtains. He finishes arranging the things in his apartment on Saturday night.

Before he goes to bed, Ken writes his name on a small piece of paper and goes down to the mailboxes at the entrance to the apartments. He puts the paper on the mailbox for apartment 409.

Now the postman can put my letters in the right box, he thinks.

Ken looks at the box for apartment 408. The name on the box is Kaori Ishida.

My neighbour is a woman, thinks Ken. *I hope she is pretty and friendly. I don't know anyone in this city. I hope I can make some new friends.*

On Sunday morning, Ken cooks breakfast, and sits at his small table to eat it. He looks around the room.

It looks very nice, he thinks. *But I need some pictures on the walls. Then it will be perfect. I will go out and buy a picture today.*

Ken walks to the shopping centre, and looks in all the stores. He finds a poster in a video games store. The poster shows the characters from Ken's favourite Play Station action game.

That will look good on the wall of my apartment, he thinks. *I will hang it above my table next to the kitchen area.*

Ken cannot use tape on the walls of his apartment so he also buys a poster hanger.

When Ken gets back to his apartment, he moves the table so he can hang the poster.

How high shall I hang it? He looks at the wall. *That's strange,* he thinks. *There's a small hole in the wall!*

He puts his eye to the hole.

I can see into the next apartment! Kaori Ishida lives in the next apartment. I should not look into her apartment, thinks Ken. *It is very bad.*

He hangs the poster over the hole. He puts the table back.

I'll go for a bike ride and see the city, he thinks. *When I come back, I will play video games. I have to work tomorrow.*

Ken likes his new job, but he is lonely. All the people in the office of the car company are very nice, but they are older than him. Ken misses his family. He misses his friends from university and from his hometown. He never sees Kaori from apartment 408. He never sees any laundry on her balcony. It seems the apartment is empty.

One night in June, Ken is sitting at the table eating noodles. He is tired and bored. He doesn't want to listen to music. He doesn't want to watch TV. He doesn't want to play video games.

I want a friend! he thinks. *I want to go to a bar and chat. I want to have fun.*

Then Ken hears music. It is coming from behind the poster on the wall. He listens hard. *What is that song? I don't know it.*

Ken stands up. He moves the table very quietly. He takes the poster down. He looks through the hole in the wall.

Ken sees a woman dancing. She is wearing a long dress. It is light pink and very beautiful. She has long black hair. He can't see her face.

That must be Kaori! he thinks. *She is young. I am sure she is pretty. I want to meet her!*

The woman is a very good dancer. Ken feels happy. Ken watches her for a long time. Then the music stops, and the woman moves away. Ken can't see her any more. He feels cold and tired. He looks at the time on his smartphone.

I have been watching her for two hours! he thinks. *This is crazy. And it is wrong. I must not do it again!*

Ken puts the poster and the table back. He makes some tea and drinks it. Then he goes to bed.

The next night Ken hears the music again. He looks through the hole again. He knows it is wrong, but he can't stop.

Every night, Ken hears the music, and every night he watches the woman dancing. Sometimes she dances until midnight. Ken is always tired. He does not work well at the office. His boss is angry. Ken sometimes makes mistakes because he is sleepy. Ken tries to stop watching the dancing woman, but when she is dancing, he feels very happy. It is like a drug. He can't stop. He wants to see her face but he can never see it.

One night, Ken waits for the music to begin. But there is no music. He looks through the hole in the wall. The room is dark. He can't see anything. Ken is very sad. Ken does not hear any music for many nights. He starts living a normal life. He meets a girl. She works in the video shop. He asks her out on a date. He works hard at his job. His boss is pleased.

After three months, Ken's life is good. Then one night he hears the music again.

I will not look! he thinks. *I will not listen.*

He puts on his earphones so he can't hear the music. But it is no good. The music is different this time. It sounds angry. He takes down the poster and looks through the hole in the wall.

The woman is dancing again. She turns and Ken sees her face.

"Aaaahhhhh!" Ken shouts and falls to the floor.

The next morning, Mr Matsui is very surprised. Ken is not in the office.

Maybe he is sick, thinks Mr Matsui. He calls Ken, but Ken does not answer his phone. Mr Matsui goes to Ken's apartment. He rings the doorbell. There is no answer.

Mr Matsui is worried.

What should I do? he thinks. He calls Ken's family. They don't know anything. Mr Matsui calls the owner of the apartment building. The owner brings a key to the apartment. Mr Matsui and the owner unlock the door and go into Ken's apartment.

Ken is lying on the floor. He is dead.

The building owner calls the police. Two policemen come. One is a senior policeman, the other is very young. It is his first job.

The policemen look at Ken's body. "How did he die?" asks the young policeman.

"I don't know," says the older policeman. "But it is very strange. I came to this apartment last year. It was the same story. A man died in this apartment. He was young and healthy, but he died. The doctors did not know why. Maybe this time the doctors will find out the reason."

Mr Matsui and the building owner are waiting outside the apartment. The policemen come to talk to them. The older policeman tells them the medical team will come. Mr Matsui tells the policemen Ken's name and hometown address. The policemen say they will talk to Ken's family.

Then the younger policeman talks to the owner of the building.

"This apartment will be empty. I am looking for an apartment. Is it cheap?"

The older policeman is surprised.

"A man died in here. Why do you want to live here?"

The young policeman says, "But it is OK. I will be fine. What could happen to me...?"

STORY 5: POLLY

I was very happy last April. I had a new job in a town called Cranton. I found an apartment in a new building, next to a garden centre. I joined a golf club. I met a new boyfriend at the club. His name was Eric and he worked in a bank. Life was good.

Then, in June, Polly came to live in my apartment. After that, life was not so good. She was the worst roommate. She broke cups and plates. She took food out of the refrigerator, and threw it on the floor. She used all my perfume. She took my clothes and shoes and put them in strange places. She hated my boyfriend Eric. She did not want me to see him.

Maybe you are thinking, why did I stay with a terrible roommate? Why didn't I tell her to go?

The answer is, I tried. I tried to tell Polly to go, but she would not go.

I will tell you about Polly. Why did she come to live with me? I don't know. But I remember the day she came.

One day in June, I came home to my beautiful new apartment. It is on the second floor. I climbed the stairs, took my key out of my bag and unlocked the door. I could hear water running. I ran to the bathroom. The shower was on.

I must be crazy, I thought. *I had a shower this morning, but I didn't turn the shower off before I went to work.*

I turned the shower off. The bathroom was a mess. My towels and bathrobe were in the shower. There was water everywhere. Bottles of shampoo and conditioner were lying on the floor. The bottles were empty.

Maybe I forgot to turn the shower off before I went to work, but I didn't throw my towels into the shower, or put my expensive shampoo and conditioner on the floor, I thought.

I was very frightened. I ran through the apartment. I looked in closets, and under the bed. There was no one else in the apartment.

I looked around. My computer and television and jewellery were still there. I sat on the sofa and tried to think.

Someone came into my apartment. Someone used the shower. No one is here now. Shall I call the police? They will think I am crazy. But I am frightened. Someone must have a key to my apartment. Maybe there is another apartment in this building with the same key. Did someone make a mistake and go into the wrong apartment?

I went to the door of my apartment. It had a strong lock, but if someone had a key, they could get in. There was also a chain. I hooked the chain up. Now no one could get in. I checked all the windows. They were all locked. Then I cleaned up the bathroom. I made an omelette and tried to relax. It was only 8:30pm, but I felt very tired, so I went to bed. I fell asleep quickly, but then, about midnight, I woke up. There were loud noises coming from the kitchen. I was very scared, but I also felt angry. I walked very quietly to the door of my apartment. It was closed and the chain was still on the door. I opened the closet near the door and took out a golf club. Then I went to the kitchen. The noise was very loud. I opened the door and got a big surprise. There was no one in the kitchen, but pots and pans were flying through the air. Bang! A frypan flew out of an open cupboard and landed on the floor. Then I saw the drawer with knives, forks and spoons open. There was a loud crash. Everything fell out of the drawer onto the floor.

What was happening? I didn't know, but I was angry.

"Stop!" I shouted.

Suddenly it was very quiet. I was standing in my pyjamas next to the kitchen door, holding a golf club. I felt something or someone move past me. Something, or someone, pulled my hair.

"Ouch! That hurt!" I shouted.

I couldn't go back to bed. I cleaned up the kitchen, and put everything away. Then I put my computer on the dining table, and logged onto the Internet.

Something is happening in my apartment. It can't be a ghost. Ghosts live in old houses and in graveyards. This is a new apartment. No ghosts here. I will search the Internet, I thought.

First I searched the history of my apartment building.

Maybe something terrible happened on this land many years ago. *Maybe when they built the apartment building, they woke up some ghosts,* I thought.

I searched for the history of Cranton. I didn't find anything. There wasn't anything special about the land. There was a farm on the land before. Now there is the apartment building and the garden centre.

Then I searched for 'ghosts'. This time I was lucky. I read a website about a ghost called a poltergeist. 'Poltergeist' is a German word. It means 'noisy ghost'. Poltergeists connect to people, not places. They do strange and bad things.

I put my head in my hands.

I have a poltergeist! I thought. *What can I do about it?*

I did some more searching. It seems poltergeists often go away after a few weeks or months. Sometimes poltergeists will go away if you ask them to go.

I stood up and shouted, "Go away!" I went into every room in my apartment and shouted again, "Go away!"

It was silent. Nothing happened.

I went back to bed and tried to sleep. In the morning, everything seemed as usual. I went to work. When I came home, the apartment looked normal.

Maybe it worked, I thought. *I told the poltergeist to go away and it did. No more problems.*

Then I went into my bedroom to change into my sports clothes. I wanted to go for a run. But when I looked at my bedroom mirror, I got a shock. There was a message on the glass:

--- *"You didn't say please!"*---

I looked at the message. The words were red.

My lipstick! I thought.

I ran into all the rooms in the apartment shouting, "Go away, please!"

When I got back to my bedroom, an extra word appeared on the mirror. I watched the lipstick moving. The word was --- *"No!"*---

You will think I am a little crazy, but I decided to try and live with my poltergeist.

I thought, I will be nice, and then the problem will go away.

Maybe the poltergeist is lonely. I am sure it is a woman. I will call her Polly. I will talk to her. The reports on the Internet said poltergeists don't hurt people, and usually go away after a while. So I will try that.

So I started to live with Polly. She was always there. Sometimes she was very quiet and didn't do anything. Other times, I think she was bored. Then she took my clothes out and put them on the bed. She turned on the shower and turned on the taps in the kitchen. I talked to her all the time. I told her about work. I told her about the golf club. I talked about Eric. When I talked about Eric, I could feel she was angry. I didn't understand why.

I always looked to see if there was a message on the mirror in my bedroom or in the bathroom. I left lipsticks near the mirror. But Polly didn't write any more messages for a few weeks.

When I went out on dates with Eric, Polly always did something bad in the apartment. One time she threw eggs on the floor. Another time, she put all my shoes in the washing machine and turned it on. This made me angry.

"Polly!" I shouted. "Please don't do that! I have no shoes to wear to work! Why do you hate Eric? Tell me!"

When I went to clean my teeth that night, there was a message on the bathroom mirror.

--- *"He has another girlfriend!"*---

"Polly? Why do you say that?" I asked. "Eric loves me. We want to get married. He doesn't have another girlfriend!"

Polly didn't answer, but the next day, when I wanted to meet Eric at the pub, I couldn't find my car keys or my mobile phone. I couldn't open the door to the apartment. Polly put my car keys and phone in the garbage. She used glue to stick the door to the door frame. I had to call a maintenance man to fix the door. It was very expensive. The maintenance man thought I was very strange.

"Why did you do that?" he asked. "Why did you put glue on your door?"

I couldn't tell him about Polly, so I said, "It was a mistake."

"Strange mistake," said the man.

After that, I had a long talk to Polly.

"Eric is coming for dinner on Saturday," I said. "You are wrong about him. He does not have another girlfriend. Please don't do anything bad. Please be nice. If you are bad I will never speak to you again!"

Polly wrote a message on the bathroom mirror.

--- *"OK! But you are wrong about him!"*---

Eric came for dinner. It was very romantic. He talked about taking a vacation to Thailand. He talked about getting married. It was a wonderful evening.

Then it was time for him to go home. He couldn't find his jacket. He couldn't find his wallet.

"It's very strange," he said. "Where are they?"

"I don't know," I answered. "I'll find them and bring them to the golf club tomorrow."

"OK," said Eric. "See you tomorrow." He kissed me good night, and went out.

"Polly!" I shouted. There was no answer.

I searched the apartment. Eric's wallet was in the coffee maker. His wallet was open. When I took it out of the coffee maker, some papers fell out. I picked them up. They were credit card receipts. It is wrong to read private things, but I read them. There were receipts for dinner for two people at expensive restaurants, flowers and chocolates. I was shocked.

He has another girlfriend, I thought.

But then I thought, *Maybe he went to the restaurant with his mother. Maybe he bought her flowers and chocolates. I must trust him.*

I put the papers back and walked into my bedroom. Eric's jacket came floating out from under the bed. It fell onto the bed. Then the invisible hand of Polly opened the inside pocket and took out a photograph. The photograph came through the air and stopped in front of my eyes. It was Eric and a woman. They were kissing, and the woman was waving one hand in the air. There was a large diamond ring on her left ring finger. An engagement ring! The photo turned over and I read the message on the back. ---*Engagement party. Eric and Melissa.*---

There was also a date – three days ago!

Eric told me he had a business trip! It wasn't a business trip! He was getting engaged to someone else.

"Why Polly! Why? He tells me he loves me. He talks about getting married!" I was very upset.

I lay down on the bed and cried a lot. I could feel a hand touching my hair. Then a message appeared on the bedroom mirror.

--- *"I'm so sorry. But some men are bad. I wanted you to know about Eric."*-

--

I finished with Eric and I stopped going to the golf club. My life was very quiet and boring. I was lonely, because Polly also disappeared from my life. I missed her. My apartment was always clean and tidy. There were no loud noises and nothing went missing, but still I missed her.

I joined a tennis club and bought a bike. I was busy and I made some nice new friends but still I missed Polly.

Why did she come to my apartment? And why did she go away? I thought. *I have forgotten about Eric, and now I should forget about Polly. That part of my life is finished.*

But Polly came back just one more time.

One weekend, three months later, I was surfing the Internet when my doorbell rang. I went to the door. There was a very handsome young man standing there. He was holding a large bunch of flowers.

"Here are the flowers you ordered," he said. "The cost is eighty-five dollars."

"I didn't order any flowers!" I said.

The young man looked surprised. "You ordered the flowers by email."

"No I didn't!" I said. "It must be a mistake!"

"Oh," said the man. "Uh, well. My name is Grant. I work at the garden centre next to these apartments. I can't take the flowers back. Can I give them to you as a present? I see you on your bike sometimes. I like cycling too. Maybe one day we could go on a ride together?"

"Yes," I said. "I would like that."

Grant pushed the flowers into my hands. "I have to go now. I will call you and we can make a date."

He went down the stairs.

I closed the door and walked back into my living room holding the flowers.

He likes me. He wanted to meet me, so he brought flowers, I thought.

I put the flowers in some water and went back to my computer. My email account was open. I looked at the sent messages. There was an email from my account to the garden centre. It was an order for the flowers. It gave my name, address and telephone number.

What is happening? I thought.

There was a small noise from my computer. A new message in my inbox. I opened it.

--- *"He's not like Eric,"*--- said the message.

There was another small noise and another message. This one said:

--- *"Writing by email is better than writing in lipstick."*---

"I don't know where you are," I shouted. "But thank you Polly!"

THANK YOU

Thank you for reading Strange Stories! We hope you enjoyed the story. (Word count: 7,937)

If you would like to read more graded readers, please visit our website
http://www.italkyoutalk.com

Other Level 1 graded readers include
A Business Trip to New York
A Homestay in Auckland
A Trip to London
Dear Ellen
Haruna's Story Part 1
Haruna's Story Part 2
Haruna's Story Part 3
Ken's Story Part 1
Ken's Story Part 2
Life is Surprising!
The Christmas Present
The Old Hospital
We Met Online

ABOUT THE AUTHOR

I Talk You Talk Press is a Japan-based publisher of language textbooks, graded readers and language learning/teaching resources.

Our team is made up of highly experienced language teachers and translators, who have all studied at least one additional language to an advanced level.

This experience enables us to design our materials from the perspective of both the teacher and the learner. We consult with both teachers and language learners when designing our textbooks and graded readers, and test our materials extensively in the classroom before publication.

We are a fast-growing press, and currently publish graded readers for learners of English. We publish new graded readers monthly.

www.ingramcontent.com/pod-product-compliance
Lightning Source LLC
Chambersburg PA
CBHW022350040426
42449CB00006B/816